T0282029

SNAKES

SNAKES

JULIANNA PHOTOPOULOS

This pocket edition first published in 2024

First published in a hardback edition in 2020

Published by
Amber Books Ltd
United House
London N7 9DP
United Kingdom

www.amberbooks.co.uk
Facebook: amberbooks
YouTube: amberbooksltd
Instagram: amberbooksltd
X(Twitter): @amberbooks

ISBN: 978-1-83886-444-6

Project Editor: Anna Brownbridge
Designer: Keren Harragan and Andrew Easton
Picture Research: Terry Forshaw

Printed in China

Contents

Introduction

Snakes don't have the best reputation – with lots of us finding these long and limbless, slithering lizards scary. But you may be surprised to learn that snakes actually fear us more than we do them. In fact, snakes will often go out of their way to avoid us. When our paths do cross, they tend to flee, or warn us to stay away, rather than fight. Their fierce stare may seem threatening but that's only because snakes do not have eyelids and cannot blink!

There are close to 4,000 different species of these scaly, cold-blooded animals slithering about on every continent except Antartica.

About 600 species are venomous, and only about 200 are able to kill or seriously harm a human.

From the worm-like threadsnakes to enormous pythons, snakes display exceptionally diverse colours, patterns and behaviours. And though all snakes use their forked tongues to smell, some have extra-special senses to help them find their prey. Some snakes then use venom, while others tightly squeeze prey to death – but almost all swallow their food whole. Come, let's explore their fascinating world!

ABOVE:
The rainbow boa (*Epicrates cenchria*) is one of the most spectacular boa species in the world. These brightly coloured snakes are found mostly in humid woodlands and rainforests of South America.

OPPOSITE:
The rough green snake (*Opheodrys aestivus*) is a non-venomous snake found in North America.

Europe

The small European continent – extending from the Arctic to the Mediterranean Sea and bordering Asia with Russia, Ukraine and Turkey – is home to at least 84 snake species. But not every country in Europe has snakes, or lots of them. For example, no snakes can be found in Ireland and Iceland, while Great Britain only has three snakes: the barred grass snake, the smooth snake and the common European adder. And as the name suggests, the latter, which is found from Great Britain to East Asia, is one of the most common snakes in Europe. However, most species on this continent belong to the largest snake family, called Colubridae, or colubrids, which are either harmless or else have venomous fangs at the back of their mouths that pose no danger to us. Only members of the Viperidae or viper family, such as the common European adder, are truly venomous with their long, front-hinged fangs. These snakes also have mesmerizing, zigzag patterns on their backs and distinctive triangular-shaped heads.

Other popular European snakes include the grass snake, noted for playing dead when threatened, and the Caspian whipsnake, which is thought to be the longest snake on this continent.

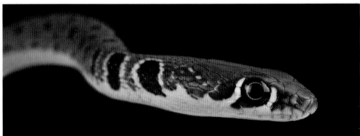

Dahl's whip snake
This harmless, *Platyceps najadum*, rarely grows over 1m (3.3ft) in length. *P. najadum* is native to Eurasia, spreading from the Balkans, Turkey and Cyprus to the Middle East, and as far as Turkmenistan and the Caucasus Mountains.

OPPOSITE:
A mass of grass snakes
The mating season, from March to June, sometimes brings grass snakes together in large groups, usually with many males writhing around the larger female. During mating, a male curls its body around a female.

ABOVE TOP AND BOTTOM:
Barred grass snake
Until 2017, grass snakes found in the United Kingdom, Switzerland, France, Italy and western Germany were considered to be the subspecies *Natrix natrix helvetica*. Now, they are a separate species called *Natrix helvetica* or barred grass snake.

RIGHT:
Grass snake
The Eurasian non-venomous species *Natrix natrix* is found near water, mainly preying on amphibians like frogs. When threatened, grass snakes are known to secrete a foul smell and taste, or play dead.

OPPOSITE (ALL PHOTOGRAPHS):

Caspian whipsnake
This species, *Dolichophis caspius*, spreads across the Balkans and parts of Eastern Europe. Its back is grey-brown, while its front is light yellow or white. At about 1.4–1.6m (4.6–5.2ft) long, the Caspian whipsnake is also known as the large whipsnake.

LEFT:

Defensive posture
Though not venomous, if threatened, the Caspian whipsnake will defend itself by raising its body, hissing loudly and pretending to attack. However, it will bite quickly and without warning if caught or stepped on.

Mating ball
These numerous entwined snakes, known as the dice snake or *Natrix tessellata*, gather together to mate in the springtime. In the summer, females lay clutches of 10–30 eggs.

18

Keeping warm
A barred grass snake basks on autumnal leaves in the British woods. After lunch, snakes usually bask to raise their body temperature, until digestion is complete. However, when temperatures start to drop, barred grass snakes search for refuge to keep their bodies warm through the winter.

OPPOSITE:
Montpellier snake
This mildly venomous juvenile snake, *Malpolon monspessulanus*, can reach up to 2m (7ft) long. Younger snakes have a conspicuous blotched or spotted pattern, including a darker pattern on the head than adults. Montpellier snakes are common throughout Spain, Portugal, the southern coast of France and northwest Africa.

LEFT TOP AND BOTTOM:
Ladder snake
Zamenis scalaris is a non-venomous species found in southwestern Europe. Only young snakes have the distinctive black ladder pattern on their backs. This pattern gradually fades and adults are left with two dark stripes running down neck-to-tail.

Western whip snake
The species *Hierophis viridiflavus* is also known as the green whip snake due to its greenish-yellow colour and irregular dark green or black bands. However, this subspecies of the western whip snake, *Hierophis viridiflavus carbonarius*, is entirely black. It is found only in southern Italy, Croatia, the Greek island of Gyaros, and Malta.

European worm snake
This blind snake, *Xerotyphlops vermicularis*, somewhat resembles an earthworm. Despite its common name, the European worm snake – or European blind snake – lives in Europe and Asia.

Armenian viper
Named after the German naturalist Gustav Radde, this subspecies, *Montivipera raddei raddei*, is common in the mountainous areas of Armenia, Azerbaijan, eastern Turkey, northwest Iran, and Turkmenistan.

Dice snake
Natrix tessellata, or the dice snake, is a harmless water snake that lives across most of Europe and Asia. Like its cousin, *Natrix natrix*, it secretes a bad smell and can play dead as a defence. Dice snakes are excellent swimmers and feed only on fish and amphibians.

European cat snake
This snake, *Telescopus fallax*, is found across the Mediterranean and the Caucasus Mountains. Though venomous, it has its fangs at the back of the upper jaw, making it difficult to inject venom into humans. Its venom, however, does work on its prey, such as lizards. It gets its name from its cat-like eyes.

RIGHT BOTTOM:

Ready to attack
The mildly venomous eastern Montpellier snake, or *Malpolon insignitus*, will defend itself if needed. When alarmed, it raises its head, flattens its neck and hisses.

OPPOSITE:

Eastern Montpellier snake
Not only can these snakes move fast, swim and climb, but they also have good eyesight. Their skin is waterproof and heatproof thanks to the liquid secreted by the two large glands located in between the eyes and nostrils.

Ottoman viper
Montivipera xanthina
is known by many
names: rock viper,
coastal viper, Turkish
viper, mountain viper
and Ottoman viper.
This aggressive and very
venomous snake has a
distinct dark brown-
black zigzag pattern on
its back. *M. xanthina*
lives in rocky and
well-vegetated habitats
across northeastern
Greece, Turkey, and
some Aegean islands.

ALL PHOTOGRAPHS:

Common European adder

This widespread venomous species, *Vipera berus*, lives across most of Europe and reaches East Asia. It can be recognized by the zigzag pattern along the back of its body and tail, the distinctive 'V' or 'X' on its head, and a dark streak from the eye to its neck. Males are grey with black markings, whilst females are usually brown with dark brown markings.

Four-lined snake

As its name suggests, the four-lined snake, or *Elaphe quatuorlineata*, has four dark stripes running down its yellowish-brown body. However, only the adults live up to this name, with juveniles having a different pattern. The non-venomous four-lined snake is one of the largest European snakes, spreading across Italy and most of Southeastern Europe.

LEFT:
Shedding
A harmless southern smooth snake, or *Coronella girondica*, sheds its skin in a process called ecdysis. As a snake's body continues to grow, its old skin layer is replaced with a new one. By rubbing against rough surfaces like rocks, the snake tears the old layer off. Snakes can shed their skin 4–12 times per year.

ABOVE:
Viperine water snake
This non-venomous snake, *Natrix maura*, can be found in rivers and lakes of southwestern Europe and northwestern Africa. Resembling its close relative, the grass snake, the viperine water snake spends most of its time in the water preying on fish and frogs.

OPPOSITE TOP:
Steppe rat snake
Named after Dione, the mother of the Greek goddess Aphrodite, *Elaphe dione* lives in eastern Europe and Asia. It is commonly known as the steppe rat snake, and has a distinctive W-shaped pattern on its head.

OPPOSITE BOTTOM:
Red whip snake
Often confused with Dahl's whip snake, this harmless colubrid species, *Platyceps collaris*, has a smaller, flatter head. *P. collaris* can reach up to 70cm (2.3ft) long in Europe, but can grow even longer (1m or 3.3ft) in Asia.

LEFT AND BELOW:
Nose-horned viper
The venomous species *Vipera ammodytes*, from southern Europe, is the most dangerous of the European vipers. It prefers rocky habitats, despite its specific name *ammodytes* meaning 'sand-diver' in Greek. Instead, its name nose-horned viper is much more apt, it having a conspicuous horn on its snout that can grow to about 5mm (0.2in).

Blotched snake

This captivating species, *Elaphe sauromates*, can grow to 2.6m (8.5ft), making it one of the largest snakes in the European continent. Young snakes have conspicuous large black-brown blotches on their backs that get fainter over time.

OPPOSITE:
Javelin sand boa
The species *Eryx jaculus* is found in Eastern Europe, the Caucasus, the Middle East and northern Africa. Unlike most snakes, it does not lay eggs but gives birth to live young that can grow to 80cm (31.5in) long.

LEFT TOP:
Milos viper
This endangered venomous viper, *Macrovipera schweizeri*, lives on four small Greek islands of the Cyclades: Milos, Sifnos, Kimolos and Polyaigos. It is often found in ravines and rocky areas with bushes, where it ambushes migratory birds.

LEFT BOTTOM:
Leopard snake
As its name suggests, the non-venomous leopard snake (*Zamenis situla*) has black-bordered reddish or brown blotches, which makes it resemble a leopard. However, it can sometimes also have stripes instead of blotches.

Africa

About 500 snake species live in Africa, the hottest and second largest continent on our planet. Africa is home to the world's largest desert, the Sahara, and to some of the most dangerous, beautiful and fascinating snakes – from small, harmless species like Peter's threadsnake to the not-so-harmless gigantic Central African rock python and the extremely venomous black mamba.

African snakes can be found in many habitats, from tropical to desert and water. To survive in this continent, snakes have evolved a number of traits: Malagasy leaf-nosed snakes' camouflage is spot on, Saharan horned vipers slither sideways across the sand, black mambas and the cryptic puff adders and boomslangs have very potent venom, and non-venomous species such as the African rock pythons have a strong grip. Some cobras can also spit to blind predators or attackers, while others, like the Egyptian cobra, can only warn them off with their hissing, large hoods and defensive displays.

Though snakes will usually try to escape when confronted, some will bite when threatened or stepped on – and people most at risk live in poor, rural regions of Africa, where it is really hard for them to get treatment.

OPPOSITE:
Ball python
This striking species, *Python regius*, is native to West and Central Africa. Commonly known as the ball python or royal python, it is the smallest African python, reaching up to 1.82m (6ft) in length. When frightened, the ball python curls into a ball.

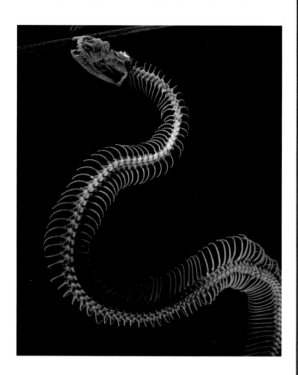

ABOVE:

Lithe skeleton

This skeleton belongs to Africa's longest venomous snake, the black mamba. Black mambas are about 2–3m (6.6–9.8ft) long and spread their cobra-like neck into a hood when alarmed. Their lithe bodies make them very fast and ready to inject venom with their 6.5mm (0.26in)-long fangs, situated in the front of the mouth.

RIGHT:

Black mamba

The lethally venomous species *Dendroaspis polylepis*, or black mamba, lives in the savannahs and rocky hills of southern and eastern Africa. Black mambas are highly aggressive and get their name from the black interior of their mouths, which they display when they are threatened.

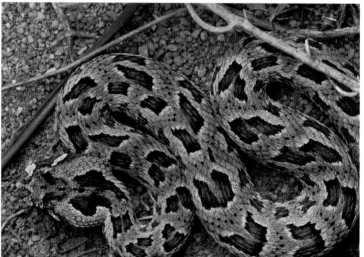

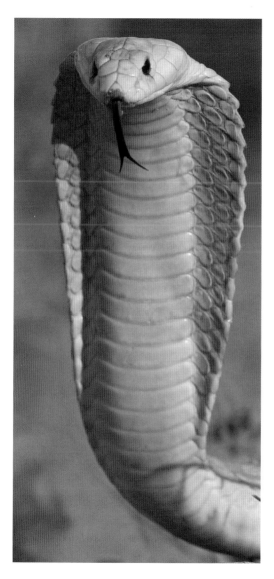

OPPOSITE TOP AND
BOTTOM:

Many-horned adder
As its common
name suggests,
the many-horned
adder, or *Bitis
cornuta*, has two
to five distinctive
horn-like scales
above both eyes. Its
back is filled with
large, dark brown
blotches, which
resemble squares or
parallelograms, with
white borders.

LEFT:

Cape cobra
Also known as the
yellow cobra, this
venomous species,
Naja nivea, actually
varies in its colour:
from yellow and
gold to brown or
even black. It lives
in a wide range
of habitats across
southern Africa.

Eastern green mamba
This elusive species (*Dendroaspis angusticeps*) gets its name from the bright green scales on its back. The green colour helps the snake blend in with its tree-dwelling environment in the coastal regions of southern East Africa. Young snakes, however, are blue-green and become bright green when they reach about 75cm (2.5ft) in length.

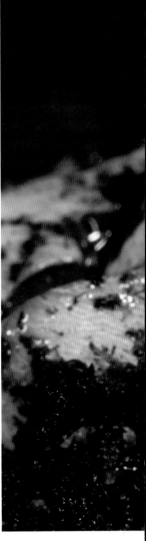

ABOVE TOP AND BOTTOM:
Boomslang
Dispholidus typus is an
extremely venomous
species from Sub-
Saharan Africa. Its
name, means 'tree
snake' in Afrikaans and
Dutch. This snake lives
mainly in forested areas
and spends most of its
time in trees.

RIGHT:
Hatchling
These big, emerald
green eyes belong to
the deadly boomslang.
At about 20cm (7.9in)
long, male hatchlings
are grey with blue
speckles, whilst the
females are brown.

Saharan horned viper
Also known as the
desert horned viper,
this venomous snake
gets its name from the
horn over each eye.
However, sometimes
some individuals don't
have horns. Saharan
horned vipers, or
Cerastes cerastes, live
in the deserts of North
Africa and parts of
Arabia and the Levant
in Western Asia.

RIGHT:
Green bush viper
As the name suggests, this venomous viper (*Atheris squamigera*) from western and Central Africa is usually a shade of green – the perfect camouflage in the forest.

BELOW:
Kenyan sand boa
Native to northern and eastern Africa, the sand boa (*Eryx colubrinus*) spends most of its time under the sand or soil.

OPPOSITE:
Hairy bush viper
Named for its bristly hair-like look, this viper (*Atheris hispida*) lives in the rainforests and bushes of Central Africa.

Central African egg-eating snake

This tree-dwelling species, *Dasypeltis fasciata*, only eats whole eggs – often several times bigger than its body! To do this, these snakes have no teeth, an extendable neck, and a flattened windpipe that can push around the egg whilst still allowing the snake to breathe.

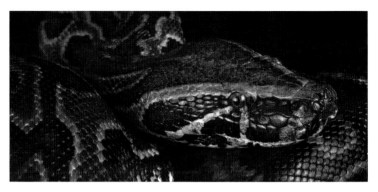

LEFT:
Squeeze
All pythons are non-venomous constrictors. This means that once they grip prey with their mouths, they wrap their coils around them and squeeze tighter every time the prey breathes out.

ABOVE TOP:
Central African rock python
The python species *Python sebae* can reach about 6m (20ft) or more, making it Africa's largest snake.

ABOVE BOTTOM:
Single gulp
An African rock python devours a gazelle. These snakes kill their prey by constriction and often eat animals up to the size of an antelope – at times, even crocodiles. They could spend weeks digesting such large animals, which are swallowed whole.

OPPOSITE:
Egyptian cobra
This large species, *Naja haje*, is one of the most venomous snakes in North Africa. With an average length of 1.4m (4.6ft), the Egyptian cobra has a stout body and a long tail. It is also known as Ouraeus – an upright snake symbol in Egyptian mythology that represented divine authority.

LEFT TOP, MIDDLE AND BOTTOM:
Egg eater
The common egg-eating snake, or *Dasypeltis scabra*, feeds exclusively on eggs. To swallow an egg, the snake holds it against its body, widens its jaws and slowly stretches the skin of its head around the egg. At the back of the throat, there are sharp protrusions that puncture the shell. The egg contents end up in the snake's belly, while the shell is expelled from its mouth.

OPPOSITE TOP AND ABOVE:
Eyelash bush viper
The Tanzanian viper *Atheris ceratophora* is known for its set of three to five horn-like scales above each eye, resembling eyelashes. Its colour can vary from a yellowish-green or olive to a grey or black, sometimes covered with markings.

RIGHT:
Malagasy leaf-nosed snake
This bizarre-looking species gets its name from the flattened, leaf-like protrusion on its snout. However, only the greyish females live up to the name, while males have a long pointed snout. Malagasy leaf-nosed snakes, or *Langaha madagascariensis*, live in the forests of Madagascar.

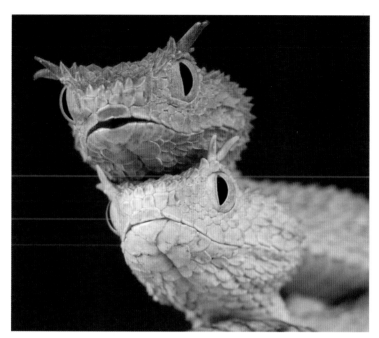

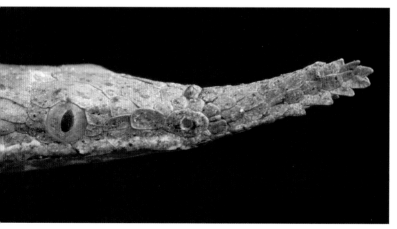

Puff adder

Don't let its gaze fool you. Found in savannahs and grasslands, this aggressive species (*Bitis arietans*) is responsible for causing the most snakebite deaths in Africa. The specific name *arietans* is derived from the Latin for 'striking violently'. When threatened, it hisses and puffs continuously and sits in an S-shaped position, ready to strike.

RIGHT TOP:

Western green mamba
This long, agile and extremely
venomous green snake,
Dendroaspis viridis, lives in
western Africa. It spends most
of its time in trees, though it
will occasionally come down
to hunt on the ground.

RIGHT MIDDLE:

Striped house snake
At about 15cm (5.9in) long,
this hatchling belongs to the
species *Boaedon lineatus* and
is known as the striped house
snake. Widespread across
Africa, females will reach
about 1m (3.3ft) in length,
whilst males rarely exceed
60cm (1.97ft).

RIGHT BOTTOM:

Yellow-bellied sea snake
As the name suggests,
this venomous snake has
a distinctive yellow belly
and a brown back. The
yellow-bellied sea snake, or
Hydrophis platurus, lives in
tropical seas around the world
except for the Atlantic Ocean.

OPPOSITE:

Southern African rock python
Known to grow to more than
5m (16ft), the species *Python
natalensis* is one of the largest
in the world. It is native
to Southern Africa, as its
common name suggests.

ABOVE TOP:
Vine snakes
Members of the
Thelotornis genus
are known as twig or
vine snakes. These are
slender, tree-dwelling
snakes with a pointed
snout and keyhole-
shaped pupils.

ABOVE BOTTOM:
Peter's threadsnake
This harmless species,
*Leptotyphlops
scutifrons*, lives
mostly underground
in countries of
Southern Africa. Peter's
threadsnakes feed on
invertebrates, especially
termites and their eggs,
and grow to about
20cm (7.9in).

OPPOSITE:
Madagascar tree boa
The beautiful
non-venomous
species *Sanzinia
madagascariensis*
is usually found in
trees or bushes near
water, on the island of
Madagascar. Tree boas
are born red, but their
colour changes to green
as they mature.

Rhinoceros viper
The beautiful, venomous
species *Bitis nasicornis*
is a close relative of the
Gabino viper. Both have
prominent horns, but the
rhinoceros viper – also
known as the butterfly
viper – has a brighter
colour pattern and
narrower head. It lives
in the forests of West
and Central Africa.

LEFT TOP AND BOTTOM:
Gabino viper
This West African
venomous viper, also
known as the West
African Gaboon viper
and *Bitis rhinoceros*,
has two distinctive
horns on its snout
and one black triangle
under each eye.

ABOVE TOP AND BOTTOM:
Spotted bush snake
This harmless green snake with black speckles can be found in the trees of African bushes and forests, preying on lizards or treefrogs. In addition to being an exceptional climber, the bush snake, or *Philothamnus semivariegatus*, is also a good swimmer and is extremely alert.

RIGHT:
Snakeskin
A young spotted bush snake sits with its shedded skin, covered in detailed patterns, in South Africa. Snakes rub against rough surfaces to shed their old skin, which is much longer than the snake itself. The skin covers the entire scale from top to bottom.

Asia

Stretching from the eastern Mediterranean Sea to the western Pacific Ocean, Asia is the largest continent. Some of its countries are among the most populated in the world. One-third of snake species also live on this continent, including the world's longest snake, the reticulated python, and the longest venomous snake, the king cobra.

Many vibrantly coloured snakes slither about in Asia, too. These unique colours and patterns are often used to hide from predators, lure prey in, or even scare off any threats. For instance, Asian vine snakes' vivid green scales help them blend within trees, while the gold-ringed cat snake, resembling a bumblebee, scares predators away. But, in nature, eye-catching colours also warn others to stay away – usually meaning these snakes are extremely venomous, like the captivating blue Malayan coral snakes or Indonesian pit vipers.

Beautifully patterned are also the saw-scaled vipers, believed to be responsible for more human deaths than all other snake species combined. However, their venom is used to make several drugs, such as blood thinners. Asia is also home to the intriguing, mildly venomous flying or gliding snakes – dangerous only to their small prey, such as mice, birds and bats.

OPPOSITE:
Banded krait
The venomous species *Bungarus fasciatus*, with alternate black and yellow bands, black eyes and yellow lips and throat, lives in India, Southeast Asia and southern China. Reaching up to 2.7m (8.9ft) in length, it is the longest species of krait.

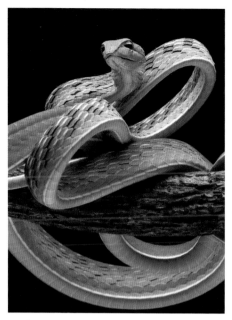

OPPOSITE AND LEFT TOP:
Asian vine snakes
The staggering members of the *Ahaetulla* genus, commonly known as Asian vine snakes, are noted for their long, slender bodies and keyhole-shaped pupils. They can be found in rainforest trees, from Sri Lanka and India to China and much of Southeast Asia.

LEFT BOTTOM:
Arabian sand boa
Also known as Jayakar's sand boa or *Eryx jayakari*, this small, harmless desert snake spends its day buried deep under the sands of the Arabian Peninsula and Iran. At dusk, it moves beneath the sand's surface, with only its eyes protruding, ready to pounce on its prey.

OVERLEAF:
Blood python
This striking non-venomous species, *Python brongersmai*, can be found in marshes and tropical swamps in the forests of Southeast Asia. Named after the blood-red markings on its skin, the blood python, or red blood python, is up and about at dusk or dawn.

RIGHT TOP:

Deadly fangs

This skeleton belongs to the longest venomous snake in the world, the king cobra, which can reach 5.5m (18ft) in length. It has two short, fixed fangs in the front of the mouth that can deliver enough venom to kill an elephant, with a single bite.

RIGHT MIDDLE:

King cobra

The threatened, venomous species *Ophiophagus hannah* lives mainly in the forests of South and Southeast Asia.

RIGHT BOTTOM:

Threat display

When disturbed, a king cobra raises its body, flares out its hood, shows its fangs and hisses – a sound almost like that of a growling dog. Despite its aggressive reputation, these snakes are shy and will avoid us whenever possible.

FAR RIGHT:

Sri Lankan pit viper

As its common name suggests, this stunning venomous snake is endemic to Sri Lanka. Its colour can vary, but usually the species *Craspedocephalus trigonocephalus* is green with a black variegated pattern, and a black line behind its eyes.

Burmese python
Among the largest species of snakes, *Python bivittatus* can reach 7m (23ft) or more in length and weigh 91kg (200lb). Burmese pythons are native to Southeast Asia and get their name from the country of Burma, now known as Myanmar. Laying clutches of up to 100 eggs, this beautifully patterned female keeps her eggs warm for two to three months, until they hatch.

RIGHT TOP AND BOTTOM:
Green pit viper species
Members of the *Trimeresurus* genus are known as green pit vipers. Though most are typically green, some species do not live up to this name, having black, or gold markings.

OPPOSITE TOP:
Striped coral snake
The venomous species *Calliophis nigrescens* spends most of its life underground in the Western Ghats of India. Commonly known as the black coral snake or striped coral snake, it comes in diverse colours and patterns.

OPPOSITE BOTTOM:
Banded Malaysian coral snake
This extremely venomous coral snake, *Calliophis intestinalis*, can be found in the forests of Southeast Asia, hunting in leaf litter at night. Its colour varies from light brown to black but has a distinctive red-orange dorsal stripe, a red tail, and its belly has a black and white pattern that it shows off when it is threatened.

Common bronzeback
The species
Dendrelaphis tristis is
a harmless, long and
slender tree-dwelling
snake. Also known as
Daudin's bronzeback or
common bronzeback,
its back is indeed a
bronze colour, helping
it hide among the trees.
Recent research has
found that members of
the *Dendrelaphis* genus
can launch themselves,
or jump, from one tree
to another.

OVERLEAF:
**Blue Malayan coral
snake**
The beautiful tropical
coral snake species,
Calliophis bivirgatus,
is native to Southeast
Asia. It is dark blue to
black – generally with
a broad blue stripe on
its sides – and has a red
head, tail and belly.
The venomous blue
Malayan coral snake
spends most of its time
amongst the leaf litter
of forests and feeds
mainly on other snakes.

Cat-eyed water snake

Found in coastal areas, especially mangroves, between western India to the eastern Philippines, the cat-eyed water snake, or *Gerarda prevostiana*, feeds almost exclusively on crabs. Instead of swallowing them whole, it tears the crab into bite-sized pieces by pulling it through its coils.

OPPOSITE:

Boulenger's bronzeback
This snake, *Dendrelaphis bifrenalis*, lives on the trees and bushes of Sri Lanka and the Eastern Ghats of South India. Named after the zoologist George Albert Boulenger, the Boulenger's bronzeback has rougher central-ridged, scales on its belly, which help it to climb trees.

LEFT AND BELOW:

Blunt-headed slug-eating snake
This small snake feeds on snails by cutting their shell with its lower jawbones, or mandibles.

LEFT:
Beware!
A mangrove snake, or
Boiga dendrophila, found
in Southeast Asia opens
its mouth wide as a threat
display. Mangrove snakes
are nocturnal and have
vertical-slit pupils like a
cat, giving it the nickname
yellow-ringed cat snake.
All members of the *Boiga*
genus have long bodies
with large heads and cat-
like eyes.

OVERLEAF BOTH PHOTOGRAPHS:
Indian cobra
Also known as the
spectacled cobra and *Naja
naja*, this venomous snake
displays a spectacular
hood when threatened.
Many Indian cobras have
two connected eye-like
markings on the back of
their hoods, resembling
eyeglasses or spectacles.

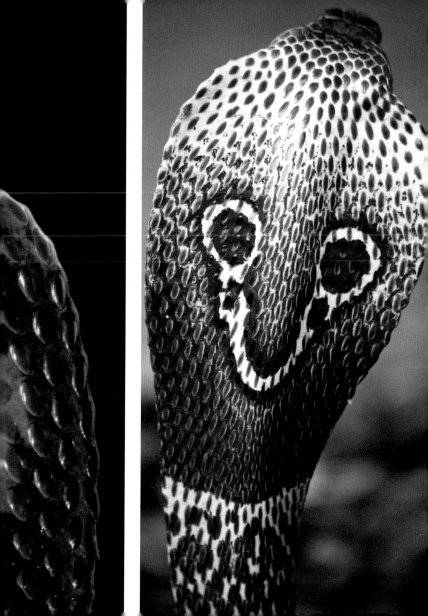

RIGHT:

Hagen's pit viper
The venomous species *Trimeresurus hageni*, from Southeast Asia, is named after the German naturalist Bernhard Hagen. It lives on trees thanks to its long prehensile tail, which it uses to grasp tree branches.

FAR RIGHT:

Caspian cobra
Also known as the Central Asian cobra, the venomous species *Naja oxiana* is native to Central Asia. For many years, it was erroneously considered a subspecies of the Indian cobra. The Caspian cobra is believed to be the most venomous species of cobra in the world.

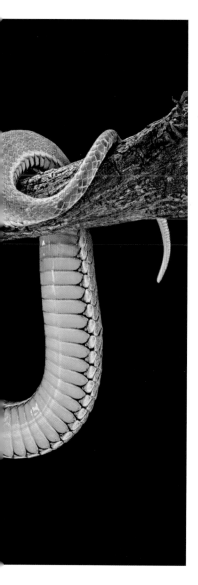
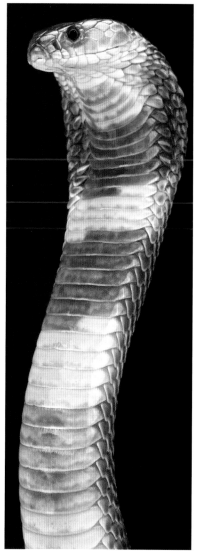

OPPOSITE:

Timor python
This non-venomous
constrictor kills its
prey by pulling it into
its ever-tightening
coils – like all pythons.
It is found in forests
and grasslands of the
southeastern islands
of Indonesia,
specifically the Lesser
Sunda Islands.

ABOVE TOP:

Painted saw-scaled viper
This well-camouflaged
species, *Echis coloratus*,
can be found in rocky
deserts (not sandy
ones)across the Middle
East and Egypt, and is
extremely venomous.

ABOVE BOTTOM
LEFT AND RIGHT:

Saw-scaled vipers
Members of the *Echis*
genus are known as
saw-scaled vipers. These
extremely venomous
vipers have a distinctive
threat display, in which
they form parallel coils
and rub their scales
together to make
a sizzling sound.

Skeleton
Without any legs or
arms, snakes have
simple skeletons.
Their skull is
attached to a long
and flexible spine,
which allows them
to bend and curl.
With hundreds of
floating ribs along
their bodies, they
can expand to the
size of their prey
– sometimes much
bigger than their
heads! This skeleton
belongs to the
Indian python.

Indian python
The large yet shy
species *Python
molurus* lives near
water in India and
several surrounding
countries. It moves
slowly, usually in
a straight line, and
rarely attacks – even
when attacked.
Often confused with
the Burmese python,
the Indian python
is usually lighter
in colour.

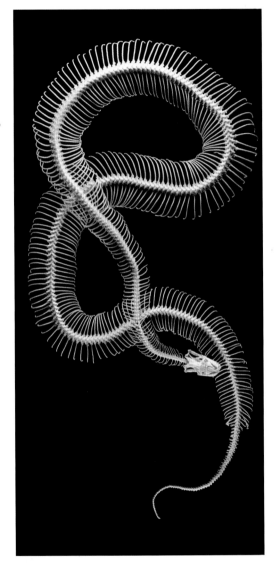

ABOVE BOTTOM:

Sand boa
Native to Iran, Pakistan
and India, the species
Eryx johnii can grow to
more than 1.22m (4ft),
making it the longest
sand boa. Its colour
varies from a yellow-tan
to a reddish brown.

ABOVE TOP AND RIGHT:

Indian rat snake
The species *Ptyas mucosa*
from South and Southeast
Asia can make a growling
sound and expand its
neck when threatened.
However, the Indian rat
snake is harmless. Even
when two males are
fighting, it looks like they
are dancing.

LEFT:

Golden tree snake

This stunning, fast-moving species, *Chrysopelea ornata*, lives in trees of South and Southeast Asia. The golden tree snake is an excellent climber and can launch itself into the air and glide, or parachute, from tree to tree.

ABOVE TOP:

Squeeze play

Golden tree snakes are mildly venomous and it takes some time to kill fast-moving prey, such as lizards and rodents. So, after sinking their fangs into their prey and injecting a dose of venom, they wrap themselves around them and squeeze to prevent them from escaping.

ABOVE BOTTOM:

Gulping down

A golden tree snake devours a large butterfly lizard. Once the prey has been killed, snakes can swallow their meal whole. This is because they can open their jaws much wider than their bodies or heads, thanks to the loosely hinged jaws, which can move independently.

OPPOSITE:
Beautiful pit viper
The extremely venomous
species *Trimeresurus venustus*
can be found only in a few
areas of Thailand.

ABOVE AND LEFT:
Fea's vipers
Members of the *Azemiops*
genus are known as Fea's
vipers, or Burmese vipers.
These rare, pitless vipers
comprise two species: *A. feae*,
or black-headed Fea's viper,
and *A. kharini* or white-
headed Fea's viper.

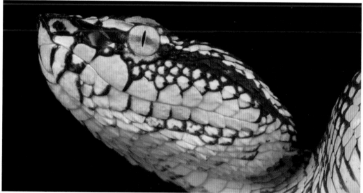

LEFT:
Indonesian pit viper
This stunningly blue, island-dwelling species, *Trimeresurus insularis*, is both aggressive and deadly. The blue variant is quite rare as, in fact, most Indonesian pit vipers are green.

ABOVE TOP:
Yellow morph
Besides blue and green, the venomous Indonesian pit viper can also be found in yellow. It lives in trees and eats birds, frogs and small mammals.

ABOVE BOTTOM:
Wagler's pit viper
Native to forests of Southeast Asia, the venomous species *Tropidolaemus Wagleri* is named after the German herpetologist Johann Georg Wagler.

RIGHT TOP:

Malayan bridle snake
The relatively small species *Lycodon subannulatus* has a slender body, resembling a horse's leather strap, or bridle. It is an excellent climber and can easily grip a tree trunk.

RIGHT MIDDLE:

Malayan krait
This species of Southeast Asia, *Bungarus candidus*, is a very venomous snake. Commonly known as the Malayan krait or blue krait, it has an alternate pattern of dark brown, black or bluish-black and yellowish-white bands on its back.

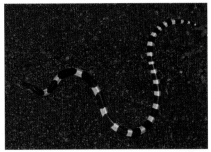

RIGHT BOTTOM:

Many-banded krait
Also known as the Chinese krait and *Bungarus multicinctus*, the many-banded krait can be found in China and Southeast Asia.

OPPOSITE:

Monocled cobra
The venomous species *Naja kaouthia* lives in South and Southeast Asia. The monocled cobra, also known as the Indian spitting cobra and monocellate cobra, has an O-shaped pattern on the back of its hood, resembling a single eye or monocellate.

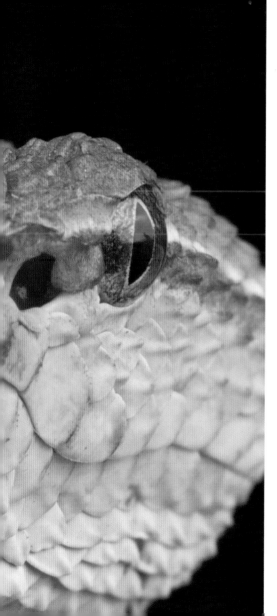

Sexual dimorphism

It is easy to distinguish between male and female Wagler's pit vipers: the green males have a relatively slender body with a large triangular head, while females are black with yellow stripes and are slightly longer than males. Here, a close-up of a male Wagler's pit viper shows its green scales and pits, or openings, between the eyes and nostril.

RIGHT:

Paradise tree snake
Also known as the paradise flying snake, this exquisite, tree-dwelling species, *Chrysopelea paradisi*, can glide 10m (33ft) or more from a treetop. It does this by flattening its body, then swinging and making snake-like movements in mid-air whilst keeping its head quite stable.

OPPOSITE:

Black-headed cat snake
The species *Boiga nigriceps* of Southeast Asian gets its name from its dark, almost black, head. However, only the adults live up to this name. Here, a red juvenile black-headed cat snake feeds on a lizard.

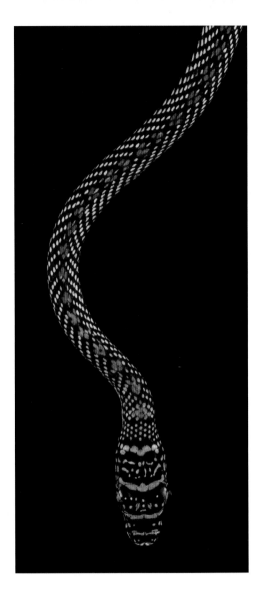

New life

At least 61cm (2ft) long, this reticulated python emerges from its egg. The watery fluid within the egg protects the snake from injury and from drying out while hatching. To break the eggshell, it uses the sharp egg tooth on its upper lip.

Vision

This dazzling orange eye with a vertical-slit pupil belongs to the reticulated python. Snakes that are active at night usually have such cat-like, or elliptical, pupils, while round pupils belong to daytime snakes. But pythons cannot see very well so have many openings lining their lips, called pit organs, which help them to 'see' the heat of their warm-blooded prey.

Reticulated python

The captivating net-like, or reticulated, patterned skin gives this python its name. It is the longest snake in the world, reaching over 6m (20ft) in length.

LEFT TOP:

Tentacled snake
Native to Southeast
Asia, the alien-looking
species *Erpeton
tentaculatum* lives
underwater and eats
fish. It is named after
its two short, scaly
tentacles protruding
from its snout, which
help it to detect prey
in muddy water.

LEFT BOTTOM:

Smooth slug snake
As the name suggests,
this southeastern Asian
snake feeds solely on
slugs and snails. More
teeth on its lower jaw
means the smooth slug
snake, or *Asthenodipsas
laevis*, can extract
snails from their shell.
A. laevis is brown and
somewhat flattened
laterally along its body.

ABOVE:

Rhinoceros rat snake
This tree-dwelling
snake is named
for its distinctive
long, rhinoceros-
like snout. The rat
snake (*Gonyosoma
boulengeri*) is
also known as the
rhinoceros snake
and Vietnamese
longnose snake.

Australia

Not to be confused with the country, Australia is the smallest and least populated continent after Antartica. But the continent – which consists of many large and small islands, including Australia, New Guinea, Fiji and other Pacific islands – has more than 170 species of snakes that live on land and in the ocean.

In fact, some of the world's most venomous snakes can be found here, most of which are members of the Elapidae family – commonly known as elapids – that have permanently erect venomous fangs. Here, elapids range from small species that live in hiding, the thickset viper-like ambush predators called death adders, to large and extremely venomous species, such as taipans, brown snakes and tiger snakes. Interestingly, Australia has no vipers and only a few colubrids, which can be venomous, or not at all.

This continent is also home to inconspicuous worm-like blind snakes and magnificent non-venomous pythons that constrict prey in their muscular coils. While the secretive and shy inland taipan is the most venomous snake in the world – one bite contains enough venom to kill almost 250,000 mice – it avoids humans and is not aggressive like its close relative, the coastal taipan.

OPPOSITE:
Green tree python
This tree-dwelling species, *Morelia viridis*, lives in New Guinea, Australia and Indonesia. Green tree pythons spend their time coiled up on branches with their heads tucked in the middle.

ALL PHOTOGRAPHS:
Belcher's sea snake
Among the most poisonous snakes, this
sea snake species (*Hydrophis belcheri*)
belongs to the Elapidae family, also
known as elapids. Members of this
family also include cobras and mambas.
H. belcheri is named after the explorer
Sir Edward Belcher, who first discovered
the snake.

King brown snake
The Australian species *Pseudechis australis* is a venomous elapid snake. Despite its common name, the king brown snake belongs to the *Pseudechis* genus known as the black snakes. Their scales have two different colour tones, giving these snakes a reticulated pattern.

LEFT:
Eastern brown snake
This true brown snake of the *Pseudonaja* genus is native to eastern and central Australia and southern New Guinea. The eastern brown snake is the second most venomous land snake in the world.

ABOVE TOP:
Black-headed python
As the name suggests, this snake's head is shiny black. The black-headed python belongs to the python family called *Pythonidae*, and is non-venomous.

ABOVE BOTTOM:
Black-naped snake
Neelaps bimaculatus gets its name from the two distinctive black patches on its head and the back of its neck. This venomous snake can be found in burrows in South and Western Australia.

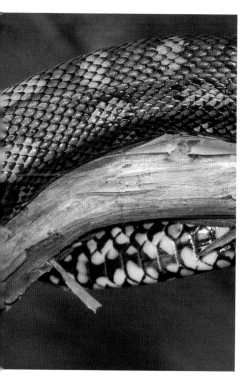

OPPOSITE BOTTOM:
In shed
A carpet python sheds its outer skin. When snakes are about to shed, their eyes look cloudy or blue, impairing their vision. This may result in aggressive behaviour.

LEFT TOP:
Carpet python
This tree-dwelling python, *Morelia spilota*, can reach a length of 2–4m (6.6–13ft) and weigh up to 15kg (33lb). It is found in Australia, New Guinea, the Bismarck Archipelago and the Solomon Islands.

LEFT BOTTOM:
Feeding
Like all members of the Pythonidae family, the carpet python is non-venomous and kills its prey by constriction. Here, a carpet python feeds on a rat, which it will swallow whole.

OVERLEAF:
Scrub python
Simalia amethistina, or the amethystine python, lives in Papua New Guinea and Indonesia. Also known as the scrub python, this snake is the largest in Papua New Guinea and can measure more than 9m (29.5ft) in length.

OPPOSITE:
Physical agility
An Australian tree snake slithers
up a tree. These slender, large-eyed
snakes can be yellow or green, black
and sometimes blue. Looking more
closely, their yellow scales on the
flanks have splashes of blue.

ABOVE:
Australian tree snake
This rare blue-coloured snake,
Dendrelaphis punctulatus, can be
found in Australia and Papua New
Guinea. It is non-venomous and goes
by many common names: Australian
tree snake, common tree snake and
green tree snake.

Bandy-bandy snakes
This Australian snake, with black and white bands along its entire body, is a member of the *Vermicella* genus. There are six species of *Vermicella*, commonly known as the bandy-bandies or hoop snakes, often recognized by their location.

Coastal taipan
One of the most
venomous snakes, the
species *Oxyuranus
scutellatus* is native
to New Guinea and
the coastal regions of
northern and eastern
Australia.

Oviparous
Coastal taipans lay
clutches of 7–20 eggs,
generally in abandoned
animal burrows.
Females can store
sperm from the males
and produce a second
clutch, often months
after mating.

Hatching time
This newly hatched
coastal taipan is 30–
34cm (12–13in) long.

On their own
These young coastal
taipans are ready to
live on their own after
hatching. It takes
around 28 months for
the females to reach
sexual maturity, while
males mature at around
16 months of age.

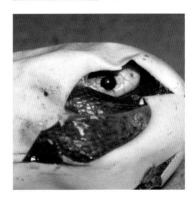

ABOVE TOP:
White-lipped snake
Native to southeastern Australia and
Tasmania, the white-lipped snake (*Drysdalia
coronoides*) gets its name from a thin white
line on its upper lip.

ABOVE BOTTOM:
Rough-scaled snake
As the name suggests, this venomous snake's
scales have a ridge down the centre, making
them rough or keeled. The rough-scaled
snake spreads from New South Wales to the
tip of Queensland, Australia.

RIGHT:
Jungle carpet python
This beautiful black and yellow python
is a subspecies of the carpet python. Known
as *Morelia spilota cheynei*, or the jungle
carpet python, it lives in the rainforests
of Queensland in Australia.

RIGHT TOP:
Dubois' sea snake
Named after Belgian naturalist Charles Frédéric Dubois, *Aipysurus duboisii* is the world's most venomous sea snake. Found in tropical waters, it lives mostly in coral reefs at sea depths up to 80m (262ft) and preys on moray eels and fish.

RIGHT BOTTOM:
Inland taipan
Oxyuranus microlepidotus, commonly known as the inland taipan, is the most venomous snake in the world. Inland taipans are reclusive and rare, usually tucked away in clay cracks and crevices of Queensland and South Australia's floodplains.

FAR RIGHT:
Southern desert banded snake
With a shovel-shaped snout, the Australian species *Simoselaps bertholdi* often buries itself in loose sand. Like all members of the *Simoselaps* genus – commonly known as the Australian coral snakes – the southern desert banded snake, or Jan's banded snake, is venomous.

Rough-scaled python

As the name suggests, this tree-dwelling python has corrugated scales. This helps the rough-scaled python (*Morelia carinata*) to climb trees and sandstone crevices. It is rare and can be found in parts of Western Australia.

OPPOSITE:
Triangular head
The rough-scaled python, or *Morelia carinata*, is usually dark brown with light brown blotches and has a triangular head and narrow neck. It reaches about 2m (6.6 ft) in length.

LEFT TOP:
Northern death adder
Though this cryptic snake resembles a viper, it actually belongs to the Elapidae family. Found in Australia and Papua New Guinea, the northern death adder (*Acanthophis praelongus*) is very venomous and lures its prey by wiggling its tail like a worm.

LEFT BOTTOM:
Red-bellied black snake
One of eastern Australia's most common snakes, the venomous red-bellied black snake (*Pseudechis porphyriacus*) is often found near shallow waters such as lagoons, hunting its main prey, frogs. In spring, males put on a fight show to win over females, and even have head-pushing contests.

ABOVE TOP:
Tongue flicking
Snakes use their tongues to gather information about their surroundings. They pick up chemical molecules from the air, which can then be 'smelled' by a pair of organs located on the roof of their mouths.

ABOVE BOTTOM:
Shelter
The ringed brown snake lives in arid shrublands and grasslands of inland Australia, from western New South Wales and Queensland to Western Australia. Here, a young ringed brown snake hides amongst tree litter.

RIGHT:
Ringed brown snake
This venomous snake (*Pseudonaja modesta*) resembles its close relative, the eastern brown snake. However, the ringed brown snake has four to seven black rings dispersed across its body. It grows up to about 50cm (20in) long.

Smooth-scaled death adder

This cryptic species, *Acanthophis laevis*, gets its shiny and glossy look from its smooth scales. The so-called smooth-scaled death adder is venomous and can inconspicuously ambush its prey. It can be found in Papua New Guinea and Indonesia.

OPPOSITE AND ABOVE:
Common death adder
The Australian species *Acanthophis antarcticus*, or common death adder, sits and waits for prey such as frogs, lizards and birds to come to it. In fact, it blends in with its surroundings and uses its grub-like tail to lure in prey, before striking and injecting its deadly venom into them.

LEFT MIDDLE AND BOTTOM:
Desert death adder
This brick-red or yellow-reddish venomous snake, with yellow bands and a flattened triangular head, can blend perfectly into its environment. It is known as the desert death adder, or *Acanthophis pyrrhus*, and lives in Australia.

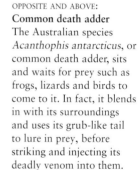

RIGHT:

Black-striped burrowing snake
At no more than 28cm (11in) long, this beautiful snake is Australia's smallest venomous snake. The black-striped burrowing snake, or *Neelaps calonotos*, is named for the black stripe on its back, which runs down its body and tail.

OPPOSITE:

Australian coral snake
Also known as the eastern shovel-nosed snake or *Brachyurophis australis*, this venomous coral snake from Australia uses its nose to dig itself into the sand. It is quite small, reaching up to 38cm (15in) in length.

ABOVE TOP:

Woma python
This Australian species, *Aspidites ramsayi*, catches most of its prey in burrows. However, due to lack of space, this requires the woma python to push a coil against the animal rather than wrapping its coils around it.

ABOVE BOTTOM AND RIGHT:

Tiger snakes
Members of the *Notechis* genus are known for their black and yellow stripes. When threatened, these venomous snakes from Australia can flatten their bodies considerably.

North America

The North American continent comprises Canada, the United States, Mexico, Central America and the Caribbean. Geographically, Greenland is also part of this continent – though no snakes roam around this island. Deserts, forests, mountains, swamps and everything in between occupy this continent, along with incredibly diverse animals. Snakes are found throughout most of North America, from the southern half of Canada down to Central America and the Caribbean.

The venomous rattlesnakes, such as the sidewinders and diamondback rattlesnakes, are only found in the Americas. These snakes are well known for making a rattling noise with the end of their tails as a warning. Some non-venomous snakes, such as the black rat snakes and gopher snakes, mimic rattlesnakes by moving their tails against the ground. The harmless and often colourful garter snakes are another species of snake living only in North America, while the eastern indigo snakes are the continent's largest native species.

The iridescent scales of rainbow boas, which refract light like small prisms and create a rainbow, will undoubtedly hypnotize you in Central and South America. And though they look like worms, the slender blind snakes or threadsnakes, are some of North America's smallest snakes.

OPPOSITE:
Checkered garter snake
The black checkerboard pattern down this greenish snake's back gives it its name. The checkered garter snake (*Thamnophis marcianus*) can be found in deserts or grasslands of southwestern United States, Mexico and Central America.

RIGHT TOP:

Milk snakes
Named after the false belief that they milked cows, milk snakes spread from southeastern Canada to South America. There are 24 subspecies of the harmless species *Lampropeltis triangulum*, many of which strikingly resemble the extremely venomous coral snakes, to scare away predators.

RIGHT BOTTOM:

Pacific gopher snake
The subspecies *Pituophis catenifer catenifer*, which has the distinctive feature of two to three rows of spots on its sides, is native to the western coast of North America.

OPPOSITE:

Black rat snake
The non-venomous species *Pantherophis obsoletus*, found in central North America, is an excellent climber. Besides this usual black colour, there is a brown-to-black variant called the Texas rat snake.

Blotched palm-pit viper
This beguiling species, *Bothriechis supraciliaris*, inhabits the mountainous area of southwestern Costa Rica. Like all members of the *Bothriechis* genus – commonly known as palm-pit vipers – it is venomous. The blotched part of its name is apt; it has irregular blotches on its back that sometimes form crossbands.

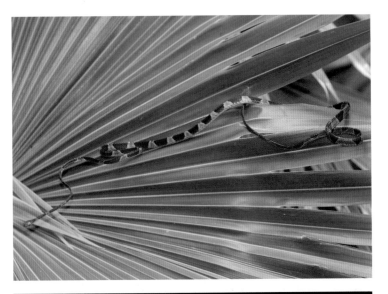

OPPOSITE TOP AND BOTTOM:
Blunthead tree snake
This long, slender, tree-
dwelling snake, with a large
head and big eyes, is known
as the blunthead tree snake
or *Imantodes cenchoa*. It can
grow to about 1.5m (5ft) long
and its large eyes make up
about a quarter of its head!

ABOVE:
Antiguan racer
Among the world's rarest, this
critically endangered species,
Alsophis antiguae, used to be
found only on a tiny private
island off the coast of Antigua
called Great Bird Island. With
conservation efforts, however,
it now also lives on the nearby
Rabbit Island, Green Island
and York Island.

Puffing snake
This non-venomous species, *Phrynonax poecilonotus*, is one of the most variable snakes in the world. Throughout its life, it continuously changes colours – from a dull colour when it hatches to a slate grey or black with yellow, orange, red or light pinkish-purple. *P. poecilonotus* lives across Mexico, Central America and South America.

RIGHT TOP:

Central American coral snake

The colourful bands of this extremely venomous snake can vary from black and red to black, red and yellow. Its snout is always black. Central American coral snakes, or *Micrurus nigrocinctus*, can be found in Mexico, Central America and South America.

RIGHT BOTTOM:

Red-tailed coral snake

As the common name suggests, the extremely venomous species *Micrurus mipartitus* has three to four red tail rings. The second ring on its head is also red, as opposed to the white bands on the rest of its body.

OPPOSITE:

Hearing

A Costa Rican coral snake slithers down a flower. Though snakes do not have external ears or eardrums like we do, their inner ears are well developed. So, while slithering away, they pick up vibrations from the ground and air through their lower jawbones and can 'hear'.

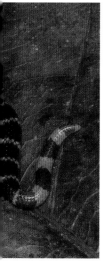

Costa Rican coral snake
Found in Nicaragua, Costa Rica and Panama, the Costa Rican coral snake (*Micrurus mosquitensis*) is deadly. It can be recognized by its distinctive yellow rings on either side of the black rings.

LEFT:
Breeding ball
Many garter males, like these red-sided garter snakes or *Thamnophis sirtalis parietalis*, often try to mate with one female, resulting in a breeding ball.

ABOVE TOP:
Garter snakes
All members of the *Thamnophis* genus are known as garter snakes. These snakes, native to North and Central America, comprise about 35 species and subspecies.

ABOVE BOTTOM:
Ovoviviparous
A female eastern garter snake, *Thamnophis sirtalis sirtalis*, gives birth to live young.

Black-speckled palm-pit viper
This distinctive emerald green
snake with black blotches
is the black-speckled palm-
pit viper or *Bothriechis
nigroviridis*. It can be found in
the mountains of Costa Rica
and Panama.

Northern Pacific rattlesnake
Crotalus oreganus, from
western North America,
comes out of its burrow. This
venomous pit viper uses the
heat-sensing pits on its face to
locate prey such as birds, mice
and rabbits.

ABOVE TOP:

Blackneck garter snake
Thamnophis cyrtopsis, or
the blackneck garter snake,
is native to southwestern
United States, Mexico and
Guatemala.

ABOVE BOTTOM:

Plains garter snake
One of the most cold-
tolerant snakes, the plains
garter snake (*Thamnophis
radix*) often basks in the sun
even on warmer winter days.

OPPOSITE:

Eastern copperhead
The venomous pit viper,
Agkistrodon contortrix, is
commonly found across the
United States and northern
Mexico. Unsurprisingly,
the copperhead gets
its name from its bronze-
hued head.

177

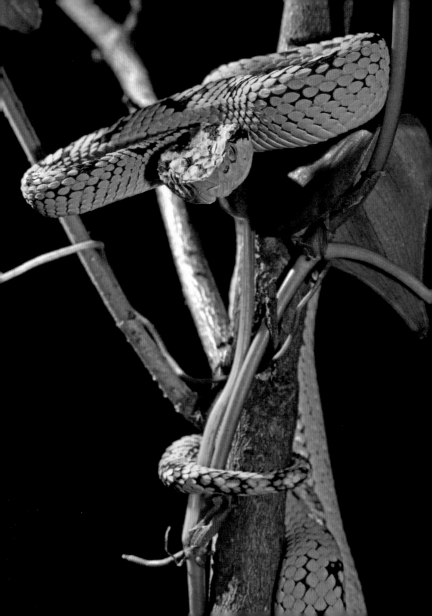

OPPOSITE:
Yellow-blotched palm-pit viper
This beautiful green snake is the yellow-blotched palm-pit viper, or *Bothriechis aurifer*. It can be found in Mexico and Guatemala, often in trees, grasping branches with its prehensile tail.

ABOVE TOP:
Northern watersnake
Northern watersnakes, or *Nerodia sipedon*, can often be seen basking on stumps, rocks and shrubs, or hunting at the water's edges during the day and at night.

ABOVE BOTTOM:
Florida green watersnake
At about 0.76–1.4m (2.5–4.6ft), *Nerodia floridana* is the longest watersnake in North America. Here, a mass of Florida green watersnakes are mating in spring.

Egg tooth
Corn snakes hatch from their eggs. About 10 weeks after a female corn snake lays a clutch of 12–24 eggs, the hatchlings use an egg tooth to break out of the shell, which is later shed. The hatchling corn snakes that emerge are about 13cm (5in) long.

ALL PHOTOGRAPHS:

Corn snakes

This stunning species of rat snake, *Pantherophis guttatus*, is found across southeastern and central United States. Often mistaken for the venomous copperhead, corn snakes are thinner, have round pupils and brighter colours, and lack heat-sensing pits. They make popular pets and through selective breeding come in a wide variety of colours and patterns.

OPPOSITE:

Prehensile tail

A beautiful tree-dwelling eyelash viper, or *Bothriechis schlegelii*, dangles from a branch. To do this, it uses its prehensile tail, which is adapted to grasp or hold.

ABOVE TOP AND BOTTOM:

Sidewinder

The rattlesnake species *Crotalus cerastes* lives in the deserts of southwestern United States and northwestern Mexico. Also known as the horned rattlesnake, its horn-like scales above its eyes prevent sand from falling into them when buried beneath it. *C. cerastes* moves quickly on sand by coiling part of its body into a loop and hurling it forwards – a method called sidewinding.

RIGHT TOP:
Eastern indigo snake
The blue-black *Drymarchon couperi* is the longest native snake in North America. Sometimes it has a reddish-orange face, like this one here.

RIGHT BOTTOM:
Brumation
In the winter, black-tailed rattlesnakes are commonly found huddling together sleeping in dens, often with other rattlesnake species, too. This activity is known as brumation and allows ectothermic or cold-blooded animals to conserve vital energy.

OPPOSITE:
Western diamondback rattlesnake
Members of the *Crotalus* genus are venomous vipers known as rattlesnakes. Like all rattlesnakes, the western diamondback rattlesnake, or *Crotalus atrox*, has a rattle at the tip of its tail, which it uses to warn off predators. Responsible for the majority of venomous snakebites in North America, they live in southwestern United States and Mexico.

ABOVE TOP:
Mexican west coast boa constrictor
Only found in western Mexico, the species *Boa sigma* is protected by locals of Sonora because they believe that it is the guardian of water.

ABOVE BOTTOM:
Mexican vine snake
This very slender snake with a prominent snout, seen from Arizona through to northern South America, can often be mistaken as a vine.

OPPOSITE:
Gray-banded kingsnake
This non-venomous snake, with orange-red and grey bands, is the gray-banded kingsnake or *Lampropeltis alterna*. It can be found across southwestern United States and Mexico.

OPPOSITE:

Brown rainbow boa
Known for its iridescent scales, the brown rainbow boa (*Epicrates maurus*) lives mainly in rainforests in southern Central America, Trinidad and Tobago, and northern South America. At night, it hunts by ambushing prey, such as mice, birds and lizards, and swallows them whole.

LEFT TOP:

Mexican west coast rattlesnake
At about 1.5m (4.9ft) or more, the western Mexican species *Crotalus basiliscus* is one of the largest rattlesnakes.

LEFT BOTTOM:

Bluestripe ribbon snake
The subspecies *Thamnophis sauritus nitae* can only be found along the northwest coast of Florida. Living near water, it is commonly known as the bluestripe ribbon snake for its two blue stripes and long, slender body that resembles a ribbon.

RIGHT TOP:

Ring-necked snake
As the common name suggests, the harmless ring-necked snake has a distinct yellow, red or yellow-orange ring on its neck. This species, *Diadophis punctatus*, curls up its tail and shows off its yellow-orange to red belly when it is threatened.

RIGHT BOTTOM:

Rubber boa
This North American species, *Charina bottae*, has a rubber-like look. Commonly known as the rubber boa, the snake is usually tan to dark brown but can also be olive-green, yellow or orange.

OPPOSITE:

Southern hog-nosed snake
Found in southeastern United States, the southern hog-nosed snake, or *Heterodon simus*, has a small, stout body and a distinctive upturned snout. When threatened, it flattens its neck and raises its head off the ground, similar to a cobra, and hisses.

ABOVE BOTTOM:
Desert rosy boa
The species *Lichanura trivirgata*, is one of the slowest-moving in the world.

ABOVE TOP:
Coastal rosy boa
Lichanura orcutti, or the coastal rosy boa, lives in rocky habitats across the southwestern parts of the United States.

LEFT:
Texas rat snake
The subspecies *Pantherophis obsoletus lindheimeri* lives mainly in Texas, but can also be found in Louisiana, Arkansas and Oklahoma. It is a brown-to-black variant of the black rat snake, often with tinges of orange or red. However, this Texas rat snake is white, or leucistic, because of a genetic mutation.

South America

The continent of South America is teeming with distinctive plants and animals. Its vast tropical rainforests make this continent one of the most biodiverse. Snakes here come in dazzling colours and patterns, like the rare checker-bellied snake, the beautiful eyelash viper, or the emerald tree boa that changes from bright red-orange to green as it ages. Whereas North America is home to the tiniest snake, the Barbados threadsnake, South America has the largest in the world – by weight.

South America's green anacondas are extraordinarily long and bulky, though their length has often been exaggerated in the past. Their relatives, yellow or Paraguayan anacondas, are also quite large. So are the non-venomous boa constrictors, which can tightly wrap around wild pigs and deer, and the venomous bushmasters. Bushmasters, along with lanceheads and rattlesnakes, are some of the most venomous snakes in this part of the world. These are part of a larger group of ambush predator snakes known as Crotalinae, or pit vipers and crotaline snakes, distinguished for their heat-sensing vision. Many young crotalines have brightly coloured tails that contrast with the rest of their bodies, which are often used to lure unsuspecting prey.

OPPOSITE:
Cryptic
This long and slender tiger rat snake, or *Spilotes pullatus*, typically lives in tall trees. Its distinctive colour pattern helps it blend in with the sunlight speckles on the trees.

Tiger rat snake
One of the largest snakes in the Americas, *Spilotes pullatus* grows to 2.7m (8.9ft) long. It spreads from southern Mexico through Central America and across most of South America to northern Argentina. It also lives in Trinidad and Tobago.

ABOVE:

Yellow-bellied puffing snake
Spilotes sulphureus is one of
largest snakes in the Americas,
reaching up to 3m (9.8ft) in
length. The yellow-bellied
puffing snake has a yellow
belly, as its name suggests, and
a yellow-greenish back. This
helps the snake stay hidden
from predators and prey
in the forests of Trinidad and
Tobago and northern
South America.

RIGHT:

Venom
The yellow-bellied puffing
snake, also known as the
Amazon puffing snake, has
developed two types of
venom that target different
prey: one for killing small
mammals, such as rats, and
another for birds and lizards.
Another mechanism, to keep
any predators away, is that
it blows up its bright yellow
throat when alarmed.

False coral snake
Also known as the calico or forest flame snake, the mildly venomous species *Oxyrhopus petolarius* lives in the forests and savannahs of Central and South America. Its teeth are located in the back of its mouth, meaning its venom is toxic to small prey but harmless to us.

ABOVE TOP AND OPPOSITE:
Heat-sensitive organs
Pit vipers, like this
two-striped forest
pitviper from South
America, have a pair of
heat-sensitive organs
located in openings, or
pits, between the eyes
and nostrils. These help
them to detect warm-
blooded prey such as
mice in total darkness.

ABOVE BOTTOM:
Variegated snail-eater
This harmless South
American species,
Dipsas variegata, spends
most of its time in trees.
It feeds on snails and
slugs, by following
them or tracking their
scent trails.

Amazon tree boa
The tree-dwelling species *Corallus hortulana*, from the Amazon, goes by many names: Amazon tree boa, macabrel and garden tree boa. It also comes in many colours and patterns, from black, grey or brown to green, yellow, orange and red, and any combination of these. Here, an Amazon tree boa sheds its old skin.

Sharp teeth
Amazon tree boas have long front teeth. This helps them grasp birds, whilst biting through the feathers. Like pit vipers and pythons, boas also have heat-sensing pit organs so that they can hunt at night.

Ready to strike
An Amazon tree boa uses its prehensile tail to hold on to the branch and take an S-shaped pose, ready to strike at its prey, such as birds, rats and bats. Though non-venomous, this species is aggressive and can attack without warning.

ABOVE TOP AND BOTTOM:
Green anaconda
Weighing up to 227kg
(500lb), this massive boa
species, *Eunectes murinus*,
is the heaviest snake in the
world. Green anacondas
spend most of their time in
water and use their long,
muscular bodies to constrict
various prey, such as turtles,
fish, deer and capybaras.

RIGHT:
Green vine snake
The long, slender species
Oxybelis fulgidus lives in
northern parts of South
America and Central
America. This tree-dwelling
snake is not to be confused
with members of the
Ahaetulla genus found in
Asia, which are also known
as green vine snakes.

RIGHT:
Checker-bellied snake
This beautiful and rare species, *Siphlophis cervinus*, lives across the Amazon rainforest of South America, as well as in Trinidad and Tobago.

BELOW LEFT, MIDDLE AND RIGHT:
New world species
These coral snakes from South America are members of the *Micrurus* genus. This is one of the genera in the Elapidae family, commonly known as elapids, which totals about 360 species of venomous snakes.

RIGHT TOP:

Common neckband snake
The species *Scaphiodontophis venustissimus* can be found across both Central and South America. It is one of the most accomplished mimickers of the venomous coral snake.

RIGHT MIDDLE:

Parrot snake
This slender snake (*Leptophis ahaetulla*), with a bright green and bronze body, lives in South and Central America.

RIGHT BOTTOM:

Southern American bushmaster
The viper species *Lachesis muta* resembles a rattlesnake. Its tail has a spiny end, which it vigorously vibrates when threatened. However, it has no rattle and gets its name *muta* from the Latin for 'mute'. At almost 3.65m (12ft) long, it is the third longest venomous snake after the king cobra in Asia and black mamba in Africa.

OPPOSITE:

Common lancehead
This easily agitated species, *Bothrops atrox*, lives in the tropical lowlands of South America. Often confused with its close relative, *Terciopelo* or *Bothrops asper*, the common lancehead usually has rectangular blotches. It can give live birth to up to 80 snakes at once!

212

ABOVE BOTTOM:
Yellow-tailed cribo
Named for its black back
with a blue glow and a
yellow tail, the indigo
snake or yellow-tailed
cribo (*Drymarchon corais*)
reaches over 2m (6.6ft) in
length. It can typically be
found in forested areas of
South America.

ABOVE TOP AND RIGHT:
Paraguayan anaconda
A close-up of the head of
the Paraguayan anaconda,
Eunectes notaeus, shows
the nostrils and eyes on the
top of its head. This is so
the snake can breathe and
see while swimming.

South American rattlesnake

This beautiful pit viper subspecies, *Crotalus durissus durissus*, lives on the coastal savannahs of Guyana, French Guiana and Suriname. It is an extremely venomous snake, and is most active at dawn and dusk, when it hunts for mainly rodents.

OPPOSITE:

Emerald tree boa

This non-venomous, reddish-orange juvenile snake will gradually turn emerald green, as its name suggests. An adult emerald tree boa, or *Corallus caninus*, closely resembles the green tree python (*Morelia viridis*) from Southeast Asia and Australia.

LEFT TOP:

Dark-spotted anaconda

Native to northeastern South America, the non-venomous constrictor *Eunectes deschauenseei* can usually be found near water. *E. deschauenseei* is named after American ornithologist Rodolphe Meyer de Schauensee.

LEFT MIDDLE:

Eyelash viper

This yellow venomous viper is named for the eyelash-like scales above its eyes. Measuring 55–82cm (22–32in) long, the eyelash viper, is relatively small. It lives in Central and South America.

LEFT BOTTOM:

Brazilian smooth snake

The giant species *Hydrodynastes gigas* can reach more than 3m (9.9ft) in length. Also known as the false water cobra, it flattens its neck into a hood like a cobra.

ABOVE TOP:
Common boa
Often confused with the boa constrictor, *Boa imperator* usually has a darker brown or red tail. It belongs to the Boidae family, known as boas or boids, which comprises non-venomous constrictors.

ABOVE BOTTOM:
Argentine boa
This subspecies, *Boa constrictor occidentalis*, is native to Argentina and Paraguay. It can only be found in the warm subtropical regions of these countries.

RIGHT:
Boa constrictor
The large, docile species *Boa constrictor* lives in tropical South America and islands in the Caribbean. In the wild, the constrictor, rarely reaches 3m (9.9ft) in length, but can grow to 5m (16ft) in captivity.

Aruba rattlesnake
As the name suggests, this rare
rattlesnake is found only on the
Caribbean island of Aruba. The
Aruba rattlesnake, or *Crotalus
unicolor*, blends in wonderfully
with its thorny scrubland and desert
habitats. It grows to about 90cm
(2.95ft) long and weighs about
1kg (2.2lb).

Credits